RECIPE FOR LEMONADE

Or

What to Do

When Life Gives You Lemons

by

April Capil

for Rachel

Nanette —
Look for the
sweetness, and
YOUR Ryan :)

P.S.: STRENGTH
IS HOT.

PART ONE:

The Stories
We Tell Ourselves

Chapter One:
Where Stories Come From

When humans first came on the evolutionary scene, we did not have the olfactory prowess (aka *smelling skills*) that other predators had, so we had to find another way to feed ourselves. What did we do? We learned how to *track* game. The process for tracking game, actually, is the same as the one we use today to solve crimes: we look for evidence, analyze our findings, and construct a story, based on what we think happened. Language, then, developed as we formed teams and learned to work together. The hunters of our early years were like the forensic scientists of *CSI*, inferring a chain of events from residual clues - putting "two and two" together to draw conclusions about the world around them.

The stories we construct, of course, are dependent - in large part - on our individual histories and perspectives. Our assumptions about future events are almost always based on our past experiences and our observances of others' past experiences. While this is helpful in many situations, it can also be *detrimental* to our development as human beings in other situations. Past experiences can preserve our safety by teaching us to, say, stay away from open flame when we've been burned before, but they can also bias us against new opportunities, like opening our heart to new people after a rough breakup.

Because of our histories, we can also make *false* assumptions, especially if we expect our future experiences to mimic our past ones. We may even go so far as to *create* future experiences that *duplicate or mimic* our previous ones, just so we can reinforce our beliefs.

Why would we do this? Fear. We don't want to be caught off guard; we don't want to be surprised or scared about our future, and convincing ourselves that we are somehow capable of *predicting* the future (as crazy as it sounds) gives us a sense of security. We tell ourselves, ***"This** city will be full of crime and rude people, just like the **last** one I lived in was,"* or *"He will cheat on me, just like my last husband did."* These assumptions are not always wrong (after all, humans do have a habit or falling into old patterns), but they are also not always right, and can be detrimental when they hold back your personal development. Always expecting your future to duplicate your past creates biases, hampering your judgment (any CSI can tell you about the perils of biased judges!)

What's important to understand is the fact that *the way we see the world depends largely on the stories we tell ourselves, based on the evidence we observe in it.*

*Note that navigating our path through the world via stories we construct is not some magical, mystical process; it is simply a pattern of behavior that we have adopted because of the way we evolved as a species. We make sense of the world around us by **examining evidence and telling ourselves a story that makes sense of that evidence**, based on beliefs we have about the way we think things work. These beliefs themselves are based on assumptions, which may or may not be valid, because, again, they are based on* *our expectations resulting from past experiences, and subject to bias.*

Let me give you an example: A child, when it is very young, tends to believe that its sole source of comfort is its mother's presence. Because children have limited exposure to the love of other people, they have no basis of comparison, and are likely to assume that mother's love is best. Should such a child find itself alone for an extended period of time, it might also assume (incorrectly, one would hope) that its mother is never coming back. Threatened with the possibility that its sole source of comfort is gone forever, the child becomes distraught. Based on the evidence (an empty room, its own feelings of abandonment), the child cannot imagine a future existence where *any* comfort is present, and will not be consoled.

To us, this scenario seems infantile and ignorant, *yet we act out the same play as adults* in various incarnations. We believe, at many times in our lives, that our happiness comes in one form and *one form only*. When that source of happiness is removed, we tell ourselves a story, based on the evidence around us, that there is *no possibility* for *future* happiness.

Over time, of course, children learn that mothers do come back, and that they are not the only human beings capable of providing comfort. The child (again, one would hope) might even learn methods of self-comfort, many of which are comparable to mother's. As adults dealing with bigger challenges, however, not all of us believe in - or are able to find - a comparable source of comfort or happiness if we lose our original source of it. When this happens, we often remain stuck in that moment of loss, regretting a decision made, which actually bars us from accessing any future peace of mind. We replay the moment over and over, imagining a different result.

As we will discover later in this book, it is not these events - these *"lemons"* life gives us - that keep us from enjoying our lives, but our refusal to move *past* them - and make *"lemonade"* of them - that hinders happiness. Life is not about finding a way to never get stuck with a lemon (they are, I believe, inevitable when it comes to the human condition), but about *how to make the best of one when it's handed to you.*

For now, though, let's focus on storytelling, and how we use it.

Chapter Two:
The Cases We Make

When we are children is, perhaps, the only time we see the world for what it truly is: a place where very few things are certain, where anything can be lost at any time, and our continued contentment is neither promised nor insurable. Now, because it would be understandably terrifying to wake up every day in a world like this, and not have a set of skills that allow us to function in it, our dinosaur brains learned to respond to our tenuous existence in one of two ways: **fight** or **flight**. We controlled our destiny, in our evolutionary years, by sheer instinct.

The funny thing is, even though we're not running from saber-toothed tigers anymore, we tend to still respond to present-day situations that scare or threaten us in the same way - by becoming defensive or evasive. With the development of language and the advent of storytelling, we've also developed another way to protect our sanity and make life easier to manage when we're *not* fighting or flighting: **we tell ourselves a story that makes us feel better.** *And the biggest story we tell ourselves is that the world we live in is not only predictable, but controllable.*

Now, we know in our heart of hearts, even at a very early age, that this story is not entirely true, and if we applied any rational logic to it, we would be forced to doubt its validity. The thing is, we don't want to believe in a scary, unpredictable world. We want to believe in a safe, controllable one. So what we do - actually, anytime we want to convince ourselves that something is true - is *we go on a hunt for evidence*, **so we can build a case that makes it easy to believe the story we tell ourselves**. If you look hard enough for evidence of something you want to prove, you WILL find it, and if you can't find it, you will likely fabricate it. Because we want to believe the world is predictable and controllable, even if it is magical thinking, we build our own little case for it, admitting and dismissing evidence, oftentimes regardless of its relevance or validity, in an effort to convince ourselves that what we believe is right and true. And keep in mind, we don't just do this with one story; we tell ourselves stories *every day* that we want to be true, and we build cases for those stories that help us believe them.

Case building comes pretty naturally to us because humans are storytellers. What do lawyers do, when presented with a mountain of evidence in a case? One side's lawyer picks through it. The other side's lawyer picks through it. Finally, each side presents their evidence, tells a story, and the Jury decides which story they believe the most. Usually, to make the stories more convincing, each lawyer comes up with reasons why the other lawyer's evidence isn't relevant, admissible, or otherwise worth paying attention to. They point out inconsistencies in the stories, or bridge gaps with plausible explanations.

The important thing to note here is that often, two people can work with the same evidence, and craft two completely different stories. What matters most is the fact that, **as individuals, we make a choice about what evidence we accept, and what evidence we dismiss**, and *that* is what determines the way our stories go. The choice is made based on our own individual beliefs and experiences, not on some universal, non-negotiable truth. Lastly, just because we've made a convincing case for something does NOT mean we've somehow discovered (and proved) this universal, non-negotiable truth. What's true for you is not always true for everyone else, and just because you strongly believe in it doesn't mean it's right and everyone else is wrong! It just means you've built a pretty convincing case *to yourself.* Back in the day, there was a pretty convincing case for the world being flat - a case Columbus blew open when he sailed his ship into history.

Chapter Three:
You'll See It When You
Believe It

So, we've talked about our habit of telling stories, about the most powerful story we tell ourselves - that our world is predictable and controllable - and how this story comforts us. We've also talked about the ways we choose to seek (or ignore) evidence to support our belief in that story. What we haven't talked about is all the *other* stories we tell ourselves - the hypotheses we have and the cases we make, throughout our lives, to support the other beliefs we have about the way the world works.

Whether we realize it or not, we analyze evidence and construct stories *every day*. We do it because when things happen, our habit is to come up with a hypothesis about why or how they happened. These hypotheses are based on many things: pre-conceived notions, existing belief systems, educated (and uneducated) guesses... and yes, even past experiences and facts. We then put together a story, using all this *stuff*, that not only helps us make sense of the world, but reinforces other beliefs we have about it.

For example, when someone cuts us off in traffic, we might assume he's a jerk and that karmic payback will ensue. This is based on dozens of beliefs and assumptions: that there are consequences for our actions; that there is some Higher Power in the world that sees every good and bad deed, and doles out punishment or rewards accordingly; that the person driving the other car was in control of his actions, that he saw us and chose to ignore us, and that because of his actions, he will inevitably face retribution. In a split second, we have told ourselves a story about what happened *that may have nothing to do with what actually happened.* Yes, the man may have been a jerk, and karmic retribution may ensue, but maybe, he just found out his wife was in labor, and was lost on his way to the hospital. Maybe he's usually a kind, excellent driver, but was in such a panic, he neglected to check his blind spot. We *don't* know everything, but we *think* we do.

We examine evidence, make a case, and pass judgment *in a split second*, and most of the time, it happens so fast, *we don't realize that there is a process of examination going on.* What's worse, the *more* cases we build with similar circumstances, the *less* likely we are to apply critical thinking to each *new* case, and the more likely we are to pass judgment without thoroughly (or even adequately) examining the evidence presented to us. Once we get to this point, it becomes very difficult to come to a different conclusion, even if the evidence is overwhelmingly supportive of one.

The problem is, what we end up doing, as we get better and better at quick judgments, is *fitting evidence to match our belief systems.* This is the equivalent of a detective wanting to believe someone is a murderer because of their race or the town where they live. The detective then tells himself a story about what the evidence in a case means, just so he can re-affirm some belief he has about "knowing" what a murderer is like. We call it **bias**, but it's actually more complicated than that - there is a *process* of analysis and conclusion-drawing, and it happens so fast, we don't even realize it IS a process. Like this detective, we come up with, then *retain*, these hypotheses in our head about how the world works, about what people are like, or what they want from us, or what they're going to do to us. We call this "collection of assumptions" **knowledge**, but really, they are just one story after another that we made up at some point to help us make sense of the world.

Because of the pace of the world, and the onslaught of information that we have to analyze every second of every day, very few of these stories we tell ourselves have had any critical thinking applied to them. What's more, they have been around for so long, most of us take them for granted and end up calling them "facts" instead of "stories I've been telling myself all these years." We treat these stories like unquestionable truths because *we have gotten in the habit* of never questioning their validity, and when their validity *is* actually questioned, we resist, often manufacturing or ignoring evidence so we can continue believing them!

Here's an example: have you ever ignored someone's advice, then talked yourself into believing a different truth, because it was a "truth" that you wanted to believe? Have you ever *manufactured* evidence in your head to support a belief that you couldn't support otherwise? If so, don't beat yourself up; everyone has at some point! *It's what we do as humans*, and we're really good at it, because we get a lot of practice. What's important though, is that **starting right here, right now, you make a promise to *be honest with*** *yourself,* and be fully aware in those moments when you know you are choosing to ignore or manufacture evidence.

I want to clarify: it's not *BAD* to make up stories, or manufacture evidence, or ignore advice. What matters is your *AWARENESS* of **this process**, that allows you to pick and choose what you believe about the world. Pretending that something is what it isn't *can* serve you, but only if you are consciously aware of how it can affect your reactions to events.

If you want to learn to make lemonade, you have to start by recognizing the choices you make every day to triage evidence, and how those choices affect your beliefs about the world.

Now, you might ask, *what's wrong with telling myself a story about a stranger I'll never see again?* Going back to the driver who cut us off, the real damage our assumption has done is not to the driver - he will get to where he's going and keep living his life regardless of what we think. The real damage is done to *us*, because in telling ourselves a story that has given us one more reason to be angry with the world, we have reduced the amount of goodwill we are willing to extend to our fellow man, and reduced our faith in a world where things can work out for us in a positive way.

Tell ourselves enough stories like this, and we will start collecting evidence from multiple cases to manufacture bigger ones, that support bigger beliefs. "That Guy Is A Jerk" gets thrown into the case file of, "People Who Drive SUVs Are Jerks," which then gets thrown into the case file of "People Who Live Here Are Jerks" and then, it's just one big case called "People Are Jerks." Before you know it, you have a giant case file that looks a lot like a chip on your shoulder about how the world's always screwing you over. *Believe me; the world is not always screwing you over, and the sooner you STOP looking for evidence that it is, the easier your life will be.*

Chapter Four:
Magic Pants

Do you ever feel like your life could be better? Do you harbor a tiny bit of discontentment, even in moments when life is *really good*, because you feel like there's probably *something* that could make it *even better*? Have you ever wondered why you always feel like you're *chasing* your happiness, and it always feels *just* beyond your reach? Like, every time you think you've reached it, you're only happy for a second, before that discontentment sets in, marring your enjoyment of it? It's no wonder. You've been *conditioned* to not be happy with yourself, your life, your behavior, by the messages that flood our lives day in and day out.

We are told, every day, that what we have is *not enough*. Through movies, through television, through billboards and bus stops and magazines at the checkout line, we are bombarded with the message that the life we *are* living is not the life we should be *content* with living, that we deserve *more, better, happier* lives. We are then presented with solutions offered by companies promising to give us these more, better, happier lives - in the form of eye creams, online degrees, shiny new cars, and mail-order meal plans. What's wrong with all this? The biggest thing: **implied in the message of *you deserve better* is the**

message, *because what you are/know/have right now is not good enough.* Every time you see a commercial or an ad in a magazine, the underlying message is *you are not good enough as you are, so buy this to make yourself better.* It's like a worm in a shiny apple, and it's a recipe for insecurity that can only be cured with - guess what? - consumerism. You buy and buy, and you never reach the pot of gold at the end of the rainbow, because the recording in your head, the story that you have been telling yourself is, *I need X to do better, to live better, to be better* and the underlying belief that this story reinforces is *I am not good enough as I am.*

What breaks my heart about this situation is our own denial of our goodness, our enough-ness, at the hands of people and companies that are just trying to sell toothpaste. They're not trying to cultivate a population of people who hate their teeth. They just want to give you a reason to buy their toothpaste instead of a competitor's, so their third quarter looks good to a bunch of shareholders. And I'm not saying there's anything wrong with self-improvement - with wanting to be smarter, thinner, richer or happier, with wanting to have cleaner teeth! **There is room in all of our lives for more happiness.** However, what you *must* do, if you want to achieve a state of *sustainable happiness*, is recognize and truly believe that **if you are always doing your best, there is no reason to be dissatisfied with yourself.** If every time you come to the table, you are doing the best you can, with what you have, with where you are, then give yourself a pat on the back, because **that is enough**. *YOU* ARE ENOUGH.

There's a joke I tell myself sometimes, working in retail. Women will come in and try on every running capri in our store, searching in vain for a pair that will make their legs look lean and their butt look smaller. They will ask all the sales girls to review their choices, and check the tags to see what each pair is made from - spandex, lycra, cotton, polyester. This will go on and on, and I inevitably want to say to them, *"Look, we don't sell Magic Pants, okay? We don't have any pants that are going to magic away a belly that's grown three children, or give you the butt of a Pilates instructor. We Do Not Sell Magic Pants."* Women come into our store looking for something that will make them love their bodies. If you hate your body, it doesn't matter what pants you're wearing. Pants are not Magic. They will not make you love your body.

If you want to look good in pants, here is the only magic you need: pay yourself a little compliment, recognize that you are doing the best that you can, and give yourself permission to wear something that fits you NOW. THEN, you look in the mirror, and you say, "This is the best my butt is going to look today, and that's okay." Maybe it looked better yesterday. Maybe it looks better today. Maybe it will look better tomorrow. *Instead of getting wrapped up in where you are on some imaginary scale of perfection, remind yourself: if you are doing the best you can, with what you have, right now,* **then you're doing pretty good, trust me.**

One caveat: if you're still unhappy, and you really want your butt to look smaller or tighter in a pair of pants, you will just have to eat healthier and get some exercise. There's only so much that a positive affirmation can do.

One other thing: we also get women looking for Magic Pants that they will "someday" look good in. Don't, don't, don't do this. This is just another way of making it okay to hate your present self, while you wait for some skinnier/prettier/younger self (Younger? Really? What are they, Time Machine Pants now?) to magically appear in the mirror. Don't expect a pair of pants to magnetically draw your present self into a "better you" - instead, be the best you that you can be today, and let that be enough. Tomorrow, be the best you that you can be then. That person might be stronger, or thinner, or fatter, or weaker, but if she is the best you can do in that moment, then be proud of yourself and acknowledge your awesomeness. Trust me when I say that if you are trying to fit into smaller pants, constantly subjecting yourself to trying on too-small pants is much more demoralizing that constantly tightening your belt around your old pants. *This is the secret to enjoying the present: be proud of where you've been, and look forward to where you're going.* Don't beat yourself up for not being there yet, or not being there sooner. As Byron Katie says, LOVE WHAT IS. If it's your best, it's enough.

In closing, I would just say that instead of looking for Magic Pants, make an effort to love what you are, where you are. Even if you are on a path to improvement, don't wait until tomorrow to be proud of yourself, to forgive yourself, to love yourself. When you find yourself saving your compliments for a "future you" that is somehow "better" than who you are now, STOP. Give yourself permission to be content with where you are right now, and forgive yourself if you're not where you wanted to be *yet*. Have goals and dreams, of course! Feel free to imagine a future life that is filled with more joy and happiness and contentment, but MAKE A PLAN to achieve those goals and dreams and *take steps every day to get there so you can celebrate the journey.* Always be doing your best, and your best will keep getting better, moving you towards that better you that you want to be. **That way, you can't deny your present self the celebration and appreciation it deserves *now*, for *being* on the journey.** Happiness comes in all shapes and sizes. You don't have to wait until you're thin or rich or married to be happy; you just have to give yourself permission to be happy with who you are now, with where you are now.

Chapter Five:
Plan For the Best; Just Don't
Think About the Worst

This might be the chapter where you start to hate me.
Stick with me, though, okay? I promise it will make sense later.

I believe, to a certain extent, in the principles of "Law of Attraction," and in things like vision boards and statements of intention and wish lists. Used properly, I believe these things can motivate us to "plan for the best." What they don't do, unfortunately, is prepare us to **deal with the worst**.

In case you haven't seen a movie or read a book about the Law of Attraction, here are its basic tenets:

The world is made of vibrating waves of energy - down to the tiniest molecule.

Energy and matter have a relationship that allows them to affect each other.

Human beings are capable of "transmitting" and "receiving" energy, both positive and negative.

Positive energy attracts more positive energy; negative energy attracts negative energy. Like attracts like.

Because of the relationship between energy and matter, positive energy can also attract positive matter (or events, or circumstances) and negative energy can attract negative matter (or events, or circumstances).

As such, the "Law of Attraction" states (roughly) that good or bad, whatever energy is dominant in your life will attract more of itself.

There is no "Law of Repulsion," because energy is inherently attracted to itself, regardless of its positivity or negativity. In order to "repulse" energy (or events, or circumstances), you must, effectively, starve it for attention by ignoring it or removing it from your life.

Being conscious of how you manage your positive and negative energies can give you some degree of control over your life, allowing you to "attract" more of what you want by focusing on it, whether through "setting your intentions," meditating on your desires, journaling, creating vision boards, making wish lists, etc.

Note that, although conscious attention to managing your energies is the most effective way to use the Law of Attraction to your advantage, because it IS a "Law," it is always working, regardless of our consciousness about our energies. Thus, even if we are unconsciously focusing on something, more of it (positive or negative) will come into our lives, whether we like it or not.

This all seems very - forgive the pun - *attractive*. I can have control over my circumstances just by thinking happy thoughts and surrounding myself with positive imagery? In a world that is unpredictable and uncontrollable, it almost seems too easy.

It is.

Here's the rub: according to most proponents of the Law of Attraction, we're not supposed to even **think** about the worst-case scenario, or we might "attract" it. When things don't go our way, when the world rains on our parade, *when life gives us lemons*, The Law of Attraction says that we *attracted* them, like a magnet. It's a kind of schizophrenic belief system - on the one hand, you have control over your future, because you can use this irresistible force to draw the things you want to you. On the other hand, if you have unconscious desires you're not in control of, those will flood into your life too (sometimes when I listen to proponents of the Law of Attraction, they sound a little like The Sphinx from *Mystery Men*).

The Law of Attraction says, if we aren't where we want to be in life, it's all our fault, because we didn't clarify our intentions enough, we wanted something else more, or we let some fear of success creep into our daily affirmations. A fervent devotion to this dogma, while helpful in opening us up to the possibility that our dreams can come true and encouraging us to take responsibility for our actions, just doesn't prepare us for lemons. It doesn't! It only makes us feel like we brought our misery on ourselves, and we end up hating the person in the mirror for not being a good enough manifester.

If you really want to be capable of true alchemy, of turning lead into gold, a vision board will not be enough. An intention and a meditation journal will not be enough. This may not be what you want to hear, but making lemonade out of lemons is not easy. You have to roll up your sleeves, bust out some elbow grease, and work at it every day until it becomes second nature.

That's why it's called *making* lemonade, not *manifesting* or *attracting* lemonade.

The good news is, it's not rocket science. Anyone willing to do the work can turn a lemon into lemonade.

So, are you with me?

PART TWO:

Lemons

Chapter Six:
What We Think We
Deserve

So, this might be the part where you hate me even more. And that is *OK*. I'm okay with that. I'm not trying to take away some dream you have of a better life. I'm just trying to get you to see that you can make the life you're already living *feel* better, simply by adjusting your perspective.

You know those Magic Eye pictures that just look like television static, until you shift your eyes a little, and suddenly it's a prehistoric scene with a brontosaurus? That's what this is going to be like. And what I'm hoping is that, like I did, once you see the order in the mess, you won't be able to UN-SEE it. You will be able to see the beauty and the happiness that is right here, right now, no matter what's going on outside. Once you can change your perspective at will, making lemonade becomes second nature, and that's when you really start appreciating the opportunity to be here, alive, now, no matter what happens to you.

Okay, we're almost there, so let's talk about one more thing: **What You Think You Deserve.**

All of us, I believe, have this idea about *what we think we deserve*. Whether it comes from our parents, our friends or coworkers, even our popular culture, this singular notion - that there is a life we *should* be living, that we, in fact, *have a right* to be living - controls most of our attitude towards our daily experience. If we're living the life we think we deserve to live, or something close to it, we're pretty content people. If we're *not* living the life we think we deserve to live, though, we find ourselves a) depressed, b) angry, and/or c) discouraged. We then ask ourselves WHY we aren't living that life (because, we think, there must be a *reason*), and what do we do? Being the storytellers that we are, we start to *build a case*. And what is the first thing we do when we start to build a case? We look for evidence.

Sometimes, the way we build a case, and the evidence we look for to support that case, is entirely based around a *dogma* - a belief system with rules, guidelines, and established consequences. A strong believer in Catholicism (which is one dogma) might make a case that he is not living the life he deserves to be living because God is in charge of making things harder or easier for him, and if he is "sinning" or not praying enough, or breaking any number of rules set forth in the Bible, God will withhold this "good life" that he deserves. And so, our Catholic prays more, he sins less, he goes to church... but still, he lives a life that is not as full as he wants it to be, as rich as he wants it to be, as beautiful as he wants it to be. He prays more, he sins even less, he goes to church even more, and still, life remains a challenge, never getting to a place where everything comes easily to him. He's following the rules of his dogma; what's the problem? *

Typically, when a dogma is not working out for people - when its logic does not produce the results they want - they either switch dogmas, or they re-examine the evidence and adjust it to fit their dogma. In the Catholic's case, he might get angry at God and decide that organized religion is a bunch of hooey. He might become an atheist, or a New Age crystal-worshipper, or a Pagan - all, of course, with the same intent: to gain access to the life he thinks he deserves to be living, as if the "right" religion will somehow become the combination to a safe where it's kept.

Personally, I think there are two ways to believe in a Higher Power. The first is to believe that a Higher Power is somehow more powerful than you are, but that you can, in effect, *control* its decisions by adhering to a set of rules. Sacrificing a fatted calf, in this sense, is really an attempt to control God by following His rules. Is this what you are really doing when you pray? **Rubbing a lamp to release a genie that will grant you wishes?** This kind of religion, sadly, is **self**-centered - reflecting only our own desires, focusing on those things in our lives that are not the way *we* want them, never entertaining the idea of a higher order that is not dictated by **our** desires, but by the need for balance in a large and complicated universe.

The second way to believe in a Higher Power begins with the acceptance that the world is, for the most part, uncontrollable. Initially, this recognition is terrifying, especially for a mammal running from a saber-toothed tiger (it might even be terrifying for a financial adviser who's just passed his Series 7 exam). It *is* the truth, though, and the sooner we start accepting it, the more we can appreciate our lives and the gift we have in being able to live them.

When you accept the inevitability of surrender in a world that will disappoint you (but, also amaze you) time and again, religion is no longer a dance for rain. By admitting you are not the Creator of the Universe, nor in any way in control of the Creator of the Universe, your prayers, mediations, and spiritual development can then become *attempts to find peace in life's chaos through faith.*

Let's say that our Catholic doesn't want to believe in another God. He turns to the Bible (again, looking for evidence to build his case), and he reads the Book of Job. Job faced trial after trial, losing nearly everything. Throughout it, Job is baffled. His friends say he must have done something bad, that Job should petition God. Only Elihu points out that God is God, and can do whatever He wants. God Himself finally appears and agrees, telling Job and his friends that they weren't there when He made the world, and that their job is not to tell Him what He should do, but to trust Him, because He is God.

Finishing the chapter, the Catholic might decide that the case he has been building - for why he is not living the life he wants to live - is missing a key piece of evidence: **God's will.** Perhaps the life he is living IS the life he is supposed to be living, and the sooner he accepts it, the happier he will be. ***Instead of focusing on having the life he wants, he can focus on wanting the life he has***. Instead of feeling deprived, he can feel attended to; instead of feeling like there is nothing he can do to access the life he feels he *deserves* to live, he accepts that what he thinks he deserves and what God thinks he deserves are two different things, and that his best route to happiness is to trust God to know best.

Thinking about this, you might conclude that I am saying there is no difference between accepting the world as an unpredictable, uncontrollable place, and believing that it is, in fact, controlled by the will of an unpredictable, uncontrollable Higher Power. You would be right! The Catholic has simply adjusted his dogma to fit his situation. *He has told himself a different story to make himself feel better*. It is no different than a wolf telling himself that lost grapes are sour.

If believing there is a benevolent force in the Universe, that ultimately has your long-term happiness in mind, makes it easier for you to make your way through this unpredictable, uncontrollable world, does it matter if you are "right" or "wrong"? As long as you're not hurting anyone over your dogma, as long as it gives you peace of mind and makes it easier to manage the ups and downs of life, I don't think it does! We get wrapped up in ideas of "right" and "wrong," forgetting that we may never *know* what is right and wrong. Right and wrong change every hundred years! Whether it is the truth, or some psychological construct we retain to make navigating our existence easier, believing that things happen for a reason can make dealing with lemons easier, and telling yourself a story that enables you to use your lemon to make something refreshing, like lemonade, will dilute the bitterness in your life.

Awareness about the stories you tell yourself, *especially the ones about what you think you deserve*, are the first step in changing your perspective.

Regarding our Catholic, ONE problem might be all the messages he's getting about how his life could be better. See Chapter Four ("Magic Pants").

Chapter Seven:
The Blame Game

So, we've talked about the stories we tell ourselves, about where those stories come from, and about how they affect our beliefs about the world and how it works. We've also talked about our expectations - what we think we deserve - and the idea that there are the lives we think we have a right to be living, and the lives we're *actually* living. Now, we're going to continue the conversation, and talk about how we react to disappointment when our expectations aren't met.

Most people don't want to believe that bad things happen for no reason. It makes the world a scary place to live in, doesn't it? You can live a good life, never being deliberately cruel to anyone, and your daughter can still be abducted on her way home from school, never to be seen again. It's terrifying to imagine a world with no cause and effect, because it's a world where no one can be held accountable for their actions, where no one takes responsibility for their lives or how they can influence other people's lives. It's also a world where you cannot control what happens to you, no matter how good or brave or resilient you are.

On the other end of the pendulum, there is the world we are living in now, where, it seems, no one is responsible for their own actions, but everyone is responsible for everyone else's. It is not a diner's fault she cannot feed herself safely; it is the restaurant's fault for serving too-hot beverages. It is not a disturbed man's fault that he shot and killed another man, but the fault of the junk food he ate the week prior. Certainly there are situations in the world we live in where people have extenuating circumstances, but more and more, we are getting in the habit of shifting blame.

The concept of *blame* is very attractive. It absolves a person of the responsibility to deal with a situation, and allows them to transfer that responsibility to another person or entity ("my mother," "the government," "Mother Nature," etc.). **BLAME concentrates and galvanizes all the bitterness associated with an event or situation, embedding the responsibility for that bitterness in a single place.** We can blame the mess our life has become on "being a middle child," or blame the destruction of a city on a hurricane, instead of acknowledging the dozens (and sometimes hundreds) of decisions and events that have, *together*, led us to a place of unhappiness.

What blame *doesn't* do is actually **solve** a problem, get us through a challenge, or erase what happened. *Blame is not penance.* It doesn't change the fact that something bad or hard or unfair happened; all it does is give us the *illusion* of control over our situation, so we can absolve ourselves of the responsibility of it and either a) make it someone else's problem, or b) demand compensation (again, re-affirming our belief that the world operates on a cause-and-effect basis). Also, note that we're only talking about **blame** here, because when good, easy, and just things happen, the responsibility for them is called **credit**, and while no one wants to take the *blame* for anything, everyone wants to take *credit*!

Because BLAME is so handy when it comes to consolidating and deferring responsibility for unexpected disappointments, it's one of our favorite ways to deal with lemons. When life hands us lemons, instead of making lemonade, what do we do? We look for someone to blame. Why deal with a lemon when you can toss it, like a hot potato, at someone else? It's hard work, making lemonade! Better to just add the lemon to the "Me vs. The World" Case File. And thus, the lemon, and the person (or entity) you *blame* for sticking you with it, becomes your scapegoat for everything that's wrong with your life.

The word "scapegoat," interestingly, comes from the Hebrew words *"ez ozel"* - literally, *"the goat that departs."* The "e-scape-goat," essentially. In the Bible, the story goes that two goats are presented to a priest, who casts their lots. One goat gets cooked and offered as a burnt offering. The priest takes the other goat and confesses all the sins of the people of Israel onto its head, then sets it loose in the wilderness as a sacrifice. Now, you might think, "The goat lives? How is that a sacrifice?" This is a common misconception - it's not the goat that sacrifices its life; it's the community that sacrifices the goat. The goat is allowed to escape because it takes the sins of the community with it when it goes. With its absence, it absolves them.

Now, obviously, there are some pluses and minuses to this scenario.

On the plus side, the community isn't allowed to hang onto past mistakes. When the goat leaves, their screw-ups go with it. Everyone gives themselves permission to forgive each other for their transgressions, letting go of all that emotional baggage. No blame!

On the minus side, the community can (theoretically) continue to lie to, cheat, and steal from each other, knowing that once a month, this goat is going to metaphorically evaporate their bad behavior and give them a clean slate (again, no blame!). Thanks to a little sympathetic magic, the community members are no longer personally responsible for their decisions.*

The thing is, scapegoating is kind of what we do when we blame others for the lemons in our lives - we look at the evidence (*they* sold us the car, *they* stole our husband, *they* were born at the wrong time) and make the case that it's *their* fault we don't have everything we think we deserve. **We tell ourselves a story: it's *their* fault we're unhappy**. This logic makes perfect sense to us (as, I'm sure, this whole sending-the-goat-into-the-wilderness-to-erase-our-sins scenario did to the Israelites), but as an unfortunate side effect, by *externalizing* our role in the whole transaction, *we actually believe we are no longer responsible for our own happiness*. We blame the scapegoats, and put the burden of all these lemons on them. The worst part is, when you absolve yourself of responsibility, you also deny your own power. **If you make someone else responsible for your happiness, how can you ever be happy without them?**

Make a decision, right now, to *stop blaming*. Don't blame yourself; don't blame your parents or your job or your country for the lemons in your life. **Lemons are a**

part of life. Instead of wasting time trying to figure out why you got a lemon or whose fault it is you have to deal with one, **grow up**. Take responsibility for your actions. If you see injustice, of course, bring it to light. If you're disappointed, accept it, and adjust your expectations next time. But don't make up a story in your head about what you deserve, and try to blame someone else when you don't get it. It's not their fault you're disappointed and it's not their responsibility to make you happy!

Remember, life doesn't hand you lemonade; it hands you *lemons*, and your job is to MAKE lemonade out of them.

*Obviously, I'm not trying to imply that early Israelites were heathens that were only good once a month. The metaphor I draw here is for the purpose of illustrating the difficulties present in any process that externalizes our transgressions. Absolution is a double-edged sword; on the one hand, you carry no guilt, but on the other, you carry no responsibility. A better process, in my opinion, is to accept responsibility for your mistakes ("own" them), ask forgiveness (from yourself and others), and, being conscious of what has happened in the past, commit to making better decisions in the future. Goats are, of course, optional.

Chapter Eight:
Lemons

Now, we get to the heart of it all: Lemons. What is a Lemon? Lemons are anything in life that you see as a raw deal, anything that makes you feel like you were cheated out of something better. Of course, when you maintain an idea about *the kind of life you think you deserve*, and maintain a belief that the life in your imagination is a better one than the life you're living *now*, you might be apt to look around and see a lot of lemons! You might start to see your car, your job, your family, your wife, your children - maybe even your own genetics - as things that could be better, SHOULD be better. You're in a state of constant dissatisfaction, because your life is not what you want it to be. This would be bad enough on its own, but over time, your dissatisfaction becomes resentment, and your resentment becomes anger. You start to get self-righteous about things. You tell yourself (and, sometimes, others), *"This isn't what I signed up for! I don't deserve this!"* And the next thing you know, you look around and it feels like your life is FILLED with lemons - dozens of things that didn't turn out to be what you thought they should be.

What's important right here, right now, is that you STOP, and see Lemons for what they really are: ***unexpected disappointments***. That's all. I'm not going to give you a pithy self-help acronym (like **F**alse **E**vidence **A**ppearing **R**eal = FEAR) to explain why or how lemons get dropped in your lap. *Lemons are just things you didn't see coming, and it's not unusual for a person to be faced with one, because most of us aren't psychic.*

Now, of course you can tell yourself, *I should have known.* You can say, *"It looked like a duck, it walked like a duck; I should have known it was a duck,"* but the fact is, hindsight is always 20/20. **Of course**, knowing what you know now, you can look back and tell yourself it was obvious! But cut yourself some slack. Most of us aren't one of Dionne Warwick's psychic friends. We're human. We make mistakes and we pull the wool over our own eyes when we want to believe something bad enough. **We tell ourselves stories and we want them to be true.** Sometimes they don't turn out to be. That's not part of some nefarious plot to ruin your day; that's *LIFE*.

What's also important to acknowledge is, when things don't turn out to be what you thought they should be, it's YOU who made the case for what you deserved, for what you signed up for. YOU tell yourself a story about what you *deserve*. YOU create the expectations in your life, and, when they aren't met, YOU tell yourself a story that you were cheated out of what you deserve. This is a choice YOU make, to create an arbitrary definition of happiness and then get mad when life doesn't serve up what you want. Even when someone else leads you to believe a story they're telling you, you still make a CHOICE to either believe that story or not.

Let me explain. We are sold a car by someone who tells us it's great - only in need of minor repairs, should last at least another five years. We drive the car home, and it breaks down on the way. We tow it and find out it needs major repairs and is on its last leg. *Classic Lemon*, we tell ourselves. We were screwed by the sales guy; he's a cheat and a liar.

What we ignore, in this whole interaction, is our own part in it. We *chose* to believe the salesman. We told ourselves a story that matched his story, and it turned out, *we were wrong*. It's not his fault we wrote the check and put the key in the ignition - we have free will, we make our own choices. *The best salesman in the world is still not a mind controller.* It doesn't make his behavior okay or justified (or legal, for that matter), but *if you want to make lemonade, you cannot tell yourself a lemon is someone else's responsibility, or you sacrifice your power to transform it into something better.*

Now, it's certainly NOT okay to intentionally deceive people. If you knowingly lie, if you deliberately pull the wool over someone's eyes so you can profit off their ignorance, you are not taking responsibility for your own situation. Justifying the process of taking advantage of people by telling yourself that *"suckers deserve what they get"* is just you making a case for a cop-out. Defrauding people is not the way to contentment; you're only cheating yourself by perpetuating an inauthentic life.

Now, I know lemons are frustrating. It's disappointing when something doesn't turn out to be what you hoped it would be. *But it is our own expectations that cause our suffering, not the events themselves!* When I meet someone angry because their lover died of a preventable disease, angry over the promotion that went to someone less qualified, angry over the house destroyed by a freak hurricane, I have compassion for them. Of course it's painful to be surprised by heartbreak. Of course it's hard to lose, to fall short, to be swindled. But the truth is, **that's life.** *That is life, and it is not easy all the time.*

My aunt was told by the National Guard that she could come back to her Port Sulphur home in 24 hours - 48 at the most. She packed a small bag with clean underwear and socks, and came back in two days. Nothing was left of her house but the front porch. Katrina had wiped it out in a few hours. Was it her fault for living in Louisiana? Was it the National Guard's fault for believing the weatherman? *If we could attribute blame to someone, would it bring her house back? No, of course not.*

Bad things happen. They happen to good people, all the time, without warning. That is the world we live in. But you know what? *Good things happen to people*, all the time, without warning. Life is not easy all the time, but it's not **hard** all the time either. People beat cancer. Children escape war-torn countries. Women on the verge of bankruptcy win the lottery. Men come home from war with all their limbs intact. Inexplicable miracles happen every day. Every single day. **But we're so busy counting our lemons, we never stop to count our blessings.**

Right now, remind yourself that *a lemon is not the end of the world.* It is not a barrier to your happiness, or a sign that you are doomed to persistent misfortune. No matter how many lemons come into your life, big or small, **they are all the same thing: unexpected disappointments.** Nothing more. And the sooner you can see a lemon for what it really is, the sooner you can make lemonade.

PART THREE:

Making Lemonade

Recipe For Lemonade

Making Lemonade isn't Rocket Science. There are four steps:

Juice your Lemons.

Add Water to Dilute.

Add Sweetener to Taste.

Serve Cool.

That's it. Three ingredients, a little elbow grease, and you have one of the most refreshing beverages on Earth. Best of all, you can customize it to your own palate.

Ready? Let's start with the hard part.

Chapter Nine:
Lemons

Wrapped up in a Lemon is a whole lotta stuff - the pith, the rind, the oil that comes out when you press one into a cutting board. Now, we're not Hot Dog On A Stick, so I'm not going to go into using the whole lemon to make our lemonade. What we want is the *essence* of the fruit - the "lesson in the lemon," so to speak.

Squeeze comes from the Latin, "quies," meaning "quiet" - presumably, to squeeze something is to quiet it. *Extract,* also from the Latin, means, "to draw out" (*ex-* "out" and *trahere,* "draw"). To extract the juice from a lemon, then, is to quiet it and draw out its essence by squeezing it. Then you're not messing around with the whole lemon - just the juice, which you can then dilute and sweeten until it's palatable, even refreshing.

Now, I know it's easy to just let a lemon sit around in your life. Sure, it's allowing you to harbor a kind of low-grade simmering resentment over something, but it's not overtly hurting anyone by just *sitting* there, right? Squeeze it, though, and all kinds of things can happen. Your hands could get dirty, juice could get in your eye. Plus, it's hard work, reaming lemons, and you don't even get that much juice from each one. The thing is, if you want to turn this lemon into lemonade, you need to roll up your sleeves and bring on the elbow grease. *Lemonade doesn't make itself.*

To squeeze a lemon and extract its juice (to get the lesson in the lemon) you must first ask yourself, *"What is this lemon really about? What was I expecting to get, that I didn't get? Why am I so bitter over it? Who am I blaming for this lemon? Why is it their fault? Do I think I could have somehow prevented this lemon from coming into my life? How?"*

Inevitably, you will find that what the lemon is *really* about is some case you're building for *How The World Always Screws Me*, or *Why Other People Are Better Than Me*, or *Ways That I Keep Not Being Able To Predict The Future*. Faced with the ridiculousness of the story you realize you keep telling yourself, you can then let go of the lemon and find something useful in the experience to teach you about your expectations.

Let me give you an example. Since the first time I visited Kaua'i, I had always envisioned starting a farm and sustainable education center there. After getting a Green MBA, I started an online business selling cardboard playhouses for children, and simultaneously found a property on Kaua'i that I could afford, thanks to an inheritance I had. I told myself all kinds of stories to make my dream seem well-thought out and reasonable - that my business would be successful, that the non-profit I was in conversations with would be supportive and that there was a market for the venture I envisioned. Just two months after my arrival in Kaua'i, though, the non-profit I wanted to work with lost its major donor and ended its relationship with the farm internship program I hoped to duplicate on my property. My small business faced a shipping crisis that forced me to shut it down, and the U.S. government bailed out all its overextended financial institutions, shrinking every funding alternative at my disposal. As our economy massively contracted, my home's value plummeted, and I found out that a lump I had been ignoring for months was Stage 3A breast cancer.

That year, as you can imagine, was **full** of unexpected disappointments.

I could have stockpiled my lemons - my *bum* house, my *bum* shipping company, my *bum* business partner, my *bum* government, my *bum* breast - and blamed everyone around me for my misfortune. I could have cursed my bad luck, or a God who didn't answer my prayers, or a community that didn't beat a path to my door, or a prince who didn't show up on his white horse. None of my blaming would have changed a thing about my situation.

Luckily, I finally had the sense to ask myself, "What did you expect, April?" I realized that I expected *everything to work out perfectly*. I expected, like most small business owners, that *nothing would go wrong*. And, predictably, I was bitter, because I thought I deserved for my dreams to come true overnight, like they do for everyone on TV. I was blaming myself, for not being psychic, for not having my lump removed sooner, for listening to doctors who said I had nothing to worry about. I blamed the doctors for *telling* me I had nothing to worry about. I blamed Realtors for letting me buy a house for $200,000 more than it was worth, and mortgage lenders for being stupid enough to lend me the money to do it! I was bitter because even as billion-dollar companies were getting money from the government, my small business was folding for lack of capital. Everything seemed unfair, unwarranted, and unjust. What all those lemons were really about, though, was my expectation that, if I followed the right dream, in the right place, at the right time, nothing would ever be hard in my life, ever again. *But that's just not the way life is!* Life is a roller coaster, no matter who you are. There are ups and downs, and that's what makes it an adventure. What I expected, what I thought I deserved, was all the ups, and none of the downs, and when everything went downhill, instead of reminding myself things would look up again, I got resentful and angry. In the midst of my distress, thankfully, I realized that *all I had done was tell myself a story*. I had, with that story, created expectations, and reality had fallen short of them. That was all. I wasn't dealt a bum hand - I dealt *myself* a hand, and imagined it wouldn't have *any* bad cards, and when they weren't all that great, I was (of course) disappointed. People do this every day. Every single day.

The juice from my lemon? It was this: **following your dreams is a guarantee of only one thing: you will never wonder *what if I had* (you might, of course, wonder *what if I hadn't*)?** In the end, I took comfort that, despite everything, I would never harbor resentment over choosing to *not* follow my dreams, and would never again take my health for granted.

We often find ourselves, in a moment of unhappiness, looking back on a turning point in our lives that, we imagine, could have gone a different way. Maybe it was a decision you made, or an accident that you think could have been prevented, or a person who came (or didn't come) into your life. Do you sometimes believe your life would be better, fuller, or richer, had things gone a different way? *It's important that we pay attention to the story we tell ourselves about this turning point; it shows us the lemons we are holding on to, that we are refusing to make into lemonade.*

By acknowledging that my situation was not the result of me being handed a "raw deal," by accepting that I was only where I was *because I made choices and had expectations*, and that my disappointment was only *because those expectations were not met*, I was able to forgive myself for not being psychic. I had simply told myself a story that, despite its implausibility, I wanted to be true. Sometimes, you tell yourself a story and it turns out to be true. Other times, it doesn't. Maybe you lie to yourself a lot; maybe you have unrealistic expectations. Maybe you're just doing the best with what you have, and sometimes it's enough and sometimes it's not. *But holding onto the idea that someone or something has screwed you out of a better life that you deserve will only keep you from seeing the lessons in your lemons.* Life will keep giving you lemons and you will keep not making them into lemonade, because you will forever feel you are at the mercy of fate, or other people, or a vengeful God. You will never be able to look at a lemon, see it as the unexpected disappointment that it really is, and *use it* to move on to the happiness that is possible for you in this life.

The fact is, there is no "better" life you "should" be living, in an alternate reality where you made a different choice, where things went a different way. **There is only THIS life, and you are missing the happiness you could be having here by investing your time and energy in cultivating regret.** Even people I have talked to who say they have "no regrets" admit that, in their dark hours, they think back on one decision, one moment in their life that, if they could go back, *Fantasy Island*-style, they would do differently. We only think about this moment, this decision, when we are dissatisfied. We imagine that, had it gone another way, life would be easy, free of the problems that complicate it. **Get this through your head:** NO ONE lives a life without problems. EVERYONE struggles with something, even people who appear happy and carefree.

Imagining that you would have some perfect life without this lemon in it is destructive and demoralizing, because *it allows you to maintain a scapegoat* - a vessel for all your bitterness that keeps it in your life.

What truly breaks my heart about the time we waste being resentful over this "better life" we "should" be living is that so few of us recognize that, if all lives have problems, in all universes, in all dimensions, this other life could be just as trying, just as frustrating! It is entirely possible that, had I not followed my dreams, I would have still gotten cancer, still had to close my business, still been disappointed. Maybe even more disappointed! **What makes our existence here so hard to bear is not our unmet expectations, but this delusion - that "it would be easier if I had only..."** *Of course*, when you compare your life to an imaginary "better" one, you will feel short-changed!

We forget that this "perfect/better/easier" life is a daydream, a fantasy. We talk ourselves into believing that our imaginings are truths, and instead of admitting it is only our *expectations* that fall short (and not our *lives*), we make a case that we are living the "wrong" life, the "worse" life. **This is not true, people.** *It is simply not true.* Daydreams can be a nice vacation from tough times, and can even be a motivation for goal-setting, but they are not evidence, and they should never bar you from appreciating the life you ARE living.

Chapter Ten:
Dilution (and, a Little
Delusion)

If life gives you enough lemons, you're bound to get down. And I don't mean, get down in a James Brown "Get On Up" get down kind of way. I mean, down*trodden*. Filled with despair. Hopeless. Beyond disappointed. Even after gleaning the lesson from your lemon, you might be angry - either at yourself, or the world, or at God - and unable to snap out of it. The bitterness, the sourness of the experience might feel so fresh, it stings without abatement. When you're in this place, even reminding yourself that "a lemon is just an unexpected disappointment" might fail to lift your spirits.

The thing is, you can't make lemonade with just lemon juice and sugar. It's too strong to drink straight up, even with sweetener. *You have to water it down and dilute its bitterness.* How do you do this? By widening your perspective.

When we finally get the lesson in a lemon, the realization is apt to make us feel foolish, ashamed, resentful or depressed. We start to tell ourselves the wrong kinds of stories - that we should have known better, that it was some kind of sick justice that brought a lemon into our lives, that our future will only hold *more* lemons, so we'd better get used to them. When you hear this soundtrack playing in your head, you must remind yourself that *it's just a story you're telling yourself, and it's not true.* Start looking for evidence that it's not true if you have to. Build a case that a lemon **is** just an unexpected disappointment, nothing more. It's not a sign that happiness, joy, and contentment aren't in your future.

The worst part about lemons is *this* phase - the one right after you squeeze them - because what you've distilled from them is so raw, so bitter, and so fresh, it's hard to imagine it could produce anything *palatable*, let alone *refreshing*. Our habit of gathering evidence struggles against our desire to see things differently, and it's hard to change perspective. If you look for evidence that tells you a *positive, constructive, forgiving story*, though, you **will** find it, even if it takes a while.

When life hands us a lemon, we sometimes think that it means happiness is no longer available to us, just because things didn't work out as we'd hoped. It's like we have this idea in our head of what our happiness *should* look like, and when life doesn't serve it up, we assume, not that THIS version of our happiness is no longer available to us, but that NO version of happiness is EVER going to be available to us. It sounds crazy, but we do this *all the time.*

The first step in diluting the bitterness of a lemon is convincing yourself that there isn't just ONE kind of happiness, or joy, or contentment available to you. This is a big step, and your mind will fight against it, but *if you want to make lemonade, you HAVE to believe it.* **Entertain the idea that happiness can come in more than one form, and in a form OTHER than the one you've set your heart on.**

The second step in watering down lemon juice involves... a little bit of dilution *by delusion*.

Let me explain: people have a tendency to compare themselves to other people. The thing is, we always seem to compare ourselves to people who are *more fortunate* than us - people who have more money, better jobs, younger wives, smarter kids, healthier parents.... the list goes on and on. And what happens when you compare yourself to people who have it better than you? Naturally, you feel like crap! Everything you have seems LESS impressive, LESS valuable, LESS worth having. You start to feel deprived and denied! Add a lemon to the mix and it's a recipe for bitterness and resentment.

This process, of "dilution by delusion" starts with one phrase: **"It Could Be Worse."** Now, fans of the Law of Attraction stay away from this phrase because they fear they will "attract" bad energy by thinking of how it could be worse, BUT this phrase, to be frank, *has saved my sanity, time and again!* It is a phrase that will allow you to change your perspective **in an instant.**

When you find yourself with a load of lemon juice and it seems like things can get no worse, instead of comparing yourself to people who are MORE fortunate than you, who have FEWER lemons, deliberately compare yourself to people who are LESS fortunate than you, who have MORE lemons. Don't go so far as to tell yourself that it will get worse, simply acknowledge that it COULD be worse, but it ISN'T. *Imagining* how it could be worse, you might appreciate how *good* (by comparison) you have it, lemons notwithstanding!

You might say that using your imagination to "trick" your mind into appreciating minor misfortune is nothing short of delusion... but that's exactly my point. You have already deluded yourself into thinking an unexpected disappointment is the end of the world; why not use your storytelling powers for good?!

Thus, the way to dilute bitterness (aka, *lemon* juice) is simple: put things in perspective by appreciating what IS good in your life, what you CAN be thankful for and happy about. If you cannot do this successfully, try imagining how things could be *worse* and see if that helps (but, don't go so far as to tell yourself things will GET worse, which will only depress you).

If you want to take things a step further and *cultivate an appreciation* of your life, so that lemons have a lesser effect on your peace of mind, I recommend keeping a gratitude journal: once a day, write down five things you have to be thankful for, that you cannot attribute to your own actions - *good* things, that are beyond your control. They may be as simple as lights turning green when you approached them, or finding a penny on the street, or getting an unexpected visit from a friend. Remind yourself how fortunate you are, to be who you are, where you are. There is always something you can be thankful for, even if it is only waking up this morning without a tube to feed you or help you breathe. Keep this practice and over time, you will come to see life as a series of happy accidents, instead of a litany of misery. You will start to see yourself as *blessed* instead of *cursed*.

Chapter Eleven:
La Dolce Vita

You've squeezed the lessons out of your lemons. You've watered their bitterness down by adjusting your perspective. Now, it's time to add one more ingredient: sweetness.

All of us have our own definition of "the sweet life" - some existence where work is easy and we haven't a care in the world. The wonderful thing is, you can find sweetness in your life *now*, if you look for it. You don't have to win the Lotto, or be famous, or marry a prince. The sweetness you need to transform your lemon water into lemonade is right here, all around you.

Throughout this book, I've talked about our gift for storytelling, our tendency to collect evidence, and our ability to combine the two to make cases that support our beliefs. If you think life sucks, it's not because life sucks - it's because you *believe* it sucks, and you seek out evidence to support that belief, and ignore or dismiss evidence to the contrary. The process of making lemonade out of lemons requires you to shift your mindset, to entertain new beliefs and look at the world with new eyes. You have to use your evidence-gathering skills to build *new* cases that are completely contrary to what you're used to. It may be difficult at first (old habits do die hard), but with enough practice, you *will* get good at it. This final step, the step that turns a semi-bitter tonic into sweet refreshment, will require all your investigative skills *and* the full commitment of your imagination.

Remember when I talked about how we sometimes make a case that we are living the "wrong life," the "worse life"? To make lemonade from lemons, you must make the opposite case - that you are living the "right life," the "better life". If you've gone through the process of diluting your bitterness, you will have the perspective that comes from being thankful for what you have (having "an attitude of gratitude," as they say). If you've been journaling your appreciation, you have pages of evidence that the world is a place where you are exposed to blessing after unexpected blessing. Now, you must take things a step further, and make an effort to seek out and truly relish the sweetness in your life.

You might say, *"There is no sweetness in my life. I have cancer. I'm underemployed. I'm broke, in debt, and I live in a small house in a boring town."* To that, I would say, "Wow, you're really good and finding evidence to support your belief that your life sucks. What if you used those investigative skills to find some evidence that your life **doesn't** suck, and that it is, in fact, **filled** with sweetness?" Well, then, you might look around you and see chemo nurses who work hard to make sure the four hours you have to be in Infusion Services are comfortable and stress free. You might appreciate the warmth of a blanket you're lucky enough to have, when there are people sleeping on the street in cities across America. You might look around at your $10 an hour job, and see a coworker who makes just as little as you do, but manages to make you laugh so hard you nearly pee your pants. Even a moment watching a child Rick-Rolling to "Never Gonna Give You Up" with a popsicle in his hand can make you appreciate that you have eyes to witness him, that you are able enough to have a job in a tough economy, if you let yourself.

Every time you laugh, every time you are moved experiencing the natural beauty of the world around you - a sunrise, the smell of rain, a snow-covered mountain or a clear blue sky - you have a chance to taste the sweetness of this world, and the privilege of your presence in it. Your small house, seen through refreshed eyes, might not look so disappointing, and your boring town, re-examined, might not seem so boring. They might, in fact, seem like Heaven, when you compare them to a collapsed apartment in an earthquake-ravaged Third World country like Haiti. Look for evidence that you don't have it so bad, and you'll find it. Then, look for evidence that you actually have it pretty good. *That* will be your sweetness.

Most importantly, when you catch yourself in a moment of thankfulness, *hold onto it*. ***Drink it in.*** Make it last. These moments of gratitude will sweeten your newly-adjusted perspective, but only if you really pay attention to them, and recognize them for the opportunities they are. They are sweet **because** of bitterness of the lemons life hands you.

Without sugar, lemonade is just an astringent. Without lemons, it's just sugar water. You need **both** elements to experience true refreshment. *Practice being glad for your blessings, and you will find the sweetness in your life, to balance the bitterness you have to face.* This is the path to making lemonade out of lemons.

Chapter Twelve:
Cooling Off

It started with a conversation about a club.

"Well, I don't want to go there if it's going to be a bunch of geezers sweating to the Oldies."

"It's not going to be old people! Kathy says it's Eighties Night!"

"See?! It's going to be old people!"

"It's not! Come on, it'll be fun. We can have drinks with your friend before, Kathy will be there till 10:30. Oh, but there's a $15 cover charge."

"Okay, but we can't go to drinks before because I can't spend $15 twice. I just spent $25 in the city yesterday and $300 on Xango last night."

"You spent $300 on Xango? Why?"

"I gave Gina the last of my Eleviv so I ordered two more bottles and then I got two more cases of Xango so we have it."

"Wait, we have plenty. Why would you do that?"

"I was going to send a case to Meryl as a thank you for Joe talking to Mike about the fireman thing."

"Well, do you know if she's going to drink it? 'Cause if she isn't, you're just wasting your money."

Wasting your money.

It's funny how certain phrases have the ability to take us from zero to sixty in a matter of seconds. When life hands you lemons, sometimes the only way to explain their presence in your life is telling yourself a story that YOU brought them into your life. In a twisted way, this kind of magical thinking gives us a sense of power over our lemons. We think, *"If I brought them IN, I can take them OUT."* You can't get rid of a lemon, though, even by passing it off onto someone else. *All you can do with a lemon is make lemonade.* **Your only power over lemons is what you do with them.**

My sister had been building a pretty successful business selling Xango, a whole-fruit mangosteen juice that reduces inflammation, and Eleviv, a dietary supplement that "promotes vigor" (the succinct way of saying, "improves mental clarity, increases physical energy and instills a sense of well-being"). It was a multi-level marketing business, with guidelines and rules on how to build it, and I'd just broken the biggest rule: *don't give anything away for free, because people don't value free things.* And yet, my sister had been paying for my four bottles of Xango a month since October, so I wouldn't be debilitated by joint pain caused by my clinical trial drug (Bondronat). I was being generous, I thought, just as she had been generous to me. And now, suddenly, I was tearing up, and feeling defensive.

Why do we escalate? Why is it that, even the most rational, sound-minded person can suddenly turn a conversation about doing laundry into a tirade on how their mother never loved them? It's because of all that evidence we're building, for the case called **"My Happiness Is Never Coming Back."**

We have plenty of exhibits for this case, of course: Exhibit A, "Things I Can't Do Right," and Exhibit B, "Mistakes I Can't Stop Making," and Exhibit C: "Reasons I'm A Screw-Up And Will Never Amount To Anything." Every time we get handed a lemon, every time we hand OURSELVES a lemon, either inadvertently or on purpose, and someone corrects us, we add a little piece of evidence to our case file. We open up the case file, and are suddenly face-to-face with all these stories about who we think we are, what we think we're capable of. Instead of it being a conversation about laundry, it becomes a conversation about every mistake we've ever made and how we suck because of it.

Here's the thing: *warm* lemonade doesn't refresh anything. You can dilute the bitterness of the lemon's juice by watering it down, you can find something to sweeten it up, but to be refreshed, you have to learn how to COOL (it) DOWN. When you find yourself escalating and overheating, the most important thing to do is STOP right where you are, and think a moment about the case you're building - what are you gathering evidence for?

In my case, the phrase *you're wasting your money* got added to the "Why I'm Always Going To Be Broke" case file, under the evidence, "Things I Can't Do Right," and everything my sister started saying to be helpful - how to properly introduce someone to the product, why you shouldn't give it away for free - kept getting added to the file. The evidence for *me being a moron* was piling up, and my sister didn't even know she was adding to it - she was just trying to be helpful.

Fortunately, I had the presence of mind to stop my mind running in the middle of the conversation, to take a deep breath and remind myself that I wasn't on trial. I felt myself start to overheat, start to lose my cool, and immediately recognized what I needed, what anyone trying to disprove a case needs: *evidence to the contrary.*

My friend Lisa is a brilliant mother. The thing I have seen good mothers do, so effortlessly, is *misdirection.* One time we were at a playground and her daughter, Molly, fell and skinned her knee while running with her Snow White water bottle. Headed for DefCon 4, Molly limped over to Lisa with the face all mothers dread: that red, scrunched, *I'm-About-To-Have-A-Total-Meltdown* look. Lisa let her wail for just a second, then immediately turned her attention to the water bottle, and said, *"Oh my Gosh, is Snow White okay?! Look at Snow White, is she okay?!"* Molly, hiccupping, suddenly stopped and turned to the water bottle, inspecting it. Sniffling, she turned it over, mirroring her mother's concern. Molly had completely forgotten about her knee. I looked at Lisa, mouth open, and she winked at me.

What works for kids can work for us, if we can stay present and in control of our reactions. We can't control the world; we can't control what happens to us, but we CAN control our reactions to it, by being mindful of the stories we tell ourselves, and the evidence we're gathering for the cases we're building.

I said that what I needed, to keep cool, was evidence to contradict the case I was building, the case of "Things I Can't Do Right." Most of us, finding ourselves in this situation, instinctively attempt to convince the person we're defending ourselves to that we actually DID do something right. **This is about as effective as trying to convince a child who's skinned her knee that her knee actually doesn't hurt that bad.** The knee DOES hurt. You DID do it wrong. You WERE disappointed by something you didn't expect. So admit it to yourself; admit it to the person you're talking to. *Own the lemon.* Then, so you won't have a full-on meltdown, anticipating newer, bigger, scarier lemons, immediately start looking for evidence of Things You Can Do Right *in a completely different context.*

When you're on a roll, tearing yourself down, escalating your own worry, you're like a runaway train. By changing the subject (and your objective) in your head, you force your brain to "jump the track" and give you a chance to regroup. You're like the crying child, getting carried away with the knee and the hurt and the pain, who suddenly turns a corner and sees a dinosaur with an ice cream cone. Your brain is thrown for a loop, and suddenly thinks, "Wha...?" It forgets what it was so upset about just long enough to shift focus to something else, and the next thing you know, you're on a different track. *Misdirection.* The saving grace of mothers, it's just as effective for grown-ups when used properly.

In my case, I told my sister I would talk to her before I shipped the case anywhere, and then got up and went into the kitchen to make myself a cup of tea. She, being helpful, wanted to continue the conversation, sensing an opportunity to teach me about her business, but I, sensing it would only add to my own feelings of inadequacy and ineptitude, said, *"Listen, I won't ship it, but I don't want to talk about this anymore."* Hurt and confused, she left, but I stayed, and made myself a hot chai (something I'm pretty good at). Then, I started to write, which always makes me feel smart and capable. By immediately doing two things that reminded me I was not a moron, I was able to "jump the track" and cool off.

You have to prioritize your cool. When you find yourself starting to overheat, starting to build evidence against your own goodness and possibility, you MUST STOP, immediately, and either start to build evidence to the contrary, or misdirect yourself, like a mother taking a child's attention away from a skinned knee.

Human beings are very good at making cases for things, and if you are not conscious of how you do this in your own life, you can inadvertently build a case for something you really don't want to do or be, *just because you're not aware you're doing it.*

About a half an hour later, my sister came back. *"Are we still friends?"* she said. I laughed. She had been in the other room all this time, telling herself a story that I was mad at her. "Of course, I'm just working on my book," I said. She walked over to me. *"Well, can I have a hug?"* I hugged her. "It's all right," I said, "I was just working through my own stuff." In one piece of evidence, I gave her the proof she needed that we were okay. Sometimes, it really is that simple.

True Refreshment

Making lemonade is simply this: taking an experience that disappointed you, learning from it, recognizing it for the isolated incident that it is, moving past it by looking for the sweetness of life, and keeping your cool by checking yourself when you start to overheat.

It's not rocket science, but it does take work, and attention, and being conscious of the stories you tell yourself. Lemons aren't all bad. They can teach us a lot about ourselves and our expectations. The important thing to remember is that life is an adventure - sometimes it's awesome and sometimes it's awful, but if you can make lemonade out of lemons, you will never want for refreshment.

Made in the USA
Charleston, SC
03 November 2011